POLISH
COOKING

GALLERY BOOKS
An Imprint of W. H. Smith Publishers Inc.
112 Madison Avenue
New York City 10016

INTRODUCTION

From what we hear of the food situation in Poland today, it is hard to believe that the cuisine of this land was once thought to be extravagant and excessive. Consider Christmas Eve dinner, for example. This feast was made up of 21 courses. The preparation of some of the dishes began months before the celebration and the cooking for that evening began in the early hours of the morning. In the midst of this conspicuous consumption, the Poles did not lose sight of the hospitality of the season. There was always a place set on Christmas Eve for an unexpected guest.

This hospitality extended to everyday visits as well as holiday celebrations. The Polish proverb — A guest in the home is God in the home — was taken to heart and even an unexpected guest would find tea or coffee and pastries. Our recipe for Crullers is just one traditional favorite.

Polish cuisine has throughout the nation's history been greatly influenced by the political climate. Kings and princes who ruled the land often married foreign princesses and noblewomen who brought their own ideas on food with them. Even so, there were the same traditional staples in every well-stocked Polish pantry. A look inside would have revealed kasha, or cereal grain, buckwheat being the favorite and the foundation for both sweet and savory dishes. There would be wheat and rye flours, fried and pickled mushrooms, smoked sausages, game, butter, eggs, cheese and honey for sweetening and for making mead. There would be fresh and pickled pickles, fresh cabbage and sauerkraut, beets, turnips, onions, carrots and potatoes. Supplies of parsley, caraway and poppyseed would be on the shelves alongside fresh and preserved apples, cherries and plums to use for puddings and as accompaniments to meat and game. From these ingredients, the people prepared the characteristic dishes that were part of the culture they had always known and loved.

SERVES 4

STUFFED EGGS

An inexpensive appetizer, these can also be a snack
or canapé. The filling is delicious cold, too,
so they are perfect for summer parties and picnics.

4 hard-boiled eggs
8oz cooked ham, ground
4 tbsps grated mild cheese
4 tbsps sour cream
2 tsps mustard
Pinch salt and pepper
2 tsps chopped fresh dill or chives
Dry breadcrumbs
Melted butter

1. Using a pin or egg pricker, make a small hole in the larger end of each egg.

2. Lower the eggs gently into boiling water.

3. As the eggs come back to the boil, roll them around with the bowl of a spoon for about 2-3 minutes. This will help set yolk in the middle of the whites. Allow the eggs to cook 9-10 minutes after the water re-boils.

4. Drain and place the eggs under cold running water. Allow to cool completely and leave in the cold water until ready to peel.

5. Peel the eggs, cut them in half lengthwise and remove the yolks. Combine yolks and all the remaining ingredients except the breadcrumbs and melted butter and mix well.

6. Pipe or spoon the mixture into each egg white and mound the top, smoothing with a small knife. Sprinkle on the breadcrumbs, covering the filling and the edge of the whites completely. Place the eggs in a heatproof dish and drizzle with melted butter. Place under a preheated broiler for about 3 minutes, or until crisp and golden brown on top.

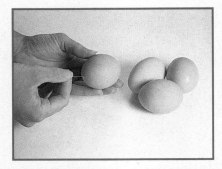

Step 1 Using an egg pricker or making a small hole with a pin in the large end of the egg will help prevent the shell from cracking.

Step 3 Use the bowl of the spoon to roll the eggs around in the boiling water to set the yolk.

Step 6 Pipe or spoon the mixture onto each egg white and mound the top.

Cook's Notes

Cook's Tip
Keeping hard-boiled eggs in water until ready to use helps prevent a gray ring from forming around the yolk.

Time
Preparation takes about 20 minutes, cooking takes about 9-10 minutes for the eggs to boil and 3 minutes for broiling.

Watchpoint
Do not broil the eggs too long. Overheating will toughen the whites.

SERVES 6

SPRING SALAD

Don't save this salad just for green — the ingredients are available all year round. Try it as a spread for sandwiches or a topping for canapes, too.

12-14oz cottage cheese
1 carrot, coarsely grated
8 radishes, coarsely grated
2 green onions, thinly sliced
Pinch salt and pepper
1 tsp chopped fresh dill or marjoram
½ cup sour cream or thick yogurt
Lettuce leaves (red oak leaf lettuce, curly endive or radicchio)

1. If cottage cheese is very liquidy, pour into a fine strainer and leave to stand for about 15-20 minutes for some of the liquid to drain away. Alternatively, cut down on the amount of sour cream.

2. Peel the carrots and shred them using the coarse side of the grater or the coarse shredding blade in a food processor. Make sure the carrots are shredded into short strips.

Step 2 Using the coarse side of a grater, grate the carrots into short strips.

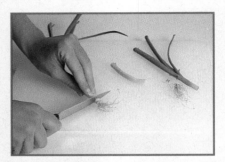

Step 3 Trim the root ends from the green onions and any part of the green tops that looks damaged.

Step 3 Use a large, sharp knife to slice through both onions at once to save time.

3. Shred the radishes with the grater and cut the onion into thin rounds with a large, sharp knife.

4. Mix all the ingredients together, except the lettuce leaves, and chill for about 20 minutes to blend all the flavors.

5. To serve, place lettuce leaves on individual plates and mound the cottage cheese salad mixture on top. If desired, sprinkle with more chopped fresh dill.

Cook's Notes

Variation
Add finely chopped red or green pepper or cucumber to the salad. If using cucumber, grate and sprinkle with salt. Leave to stand 30 minutes, rinse and pat dry.

Serving Ideas
Serve with thinly sliced whole-wheat or rye bread, lightly buttered. The salad may also be served with French bread.

Time
Preparation takes about 20 minutes and salad requires 15-20 minutes refrigeration.

SERVES 6-8

PIG'S TROTTERS IN ASPIC

Pigs were an important source of food in Poland
and no part of them was wasted. The trotters or
feet produce a stock which jells naturally.

1½lbs pig's trotters, cleaned and skinned
8oz pork or uncooked gammon, left whole
2 carrots, peeled
4 sticks celery
1 onion, quartered
2 bay leaves
5 black peppercorns
3 allspice berries
Pinch salt
6 tbsps white wine vinegar
2 egg whites
2 egg shells

1. Place the trotters, meat, carrots, celery and onion into a large stockpot.

2. Tie the bay leaves, peppercorns and allspice berries in a muslin bag and add to the pot.

3. Pour in enough water to come 2 inches above the ingredients. Bring to the boil and then simmer, covered, for 2 hours. Add more water as necessary during cooking. Skim off any foam that collects on the surface during cooking. Add salt and vinegar and cook a further 2 hours and then strain, reserving about 3 pints of the liquid.

4. Discard the muslin bag, remove meat and carrots and discard celery and onion.

5. Take the meat off the trotters and dice it along with the pork or gammon. Slice the carrot and set it aside. Strain the stock into a clean pan and add the egg whites and shells.

6. Bring to the boil, whisking constantly until a thick foam forms on top.

Step 6 Bring the liquid to the boil, whisking constantly with a large balloon whisk until a thick foam forms.

Step 7 Allow the liquid to boil up the sides of the pan and then subside. Repeat twice more.

7. Allow the stock to boil up the sides of the pan, remove from the heat and allow to subside. Allow to boil up and subside twice more, but do not whisk.

8. Strain into a clean bowl through a clean, scalded tea towel or piece of muslin. Let the foam fall into the towel and allow liquid to drain slowly through. Do not allow the crust to fall into the liquid. When the aspic is drained through, chill until syrupy.

9. Dampen a mold and pour in a thin layer of aspic. Chill in the refrigerator until firm. Place slices of carrot in a decorative pattern on top and spoon on more aspic to set the carrot. Chill again until set. Mix the meat and the remaining aspic and fill up the mold. Chill until firm, at least 4 hours. Turn out and garnish the plate with parsley if desired.

Cook's Notes

Cook's Tip
The aspic may be softened by gentle re-heating. Place the bowl in another bowl or pan of hot water. Do not stir too much or bubbles will form.

Watchpoint
If the aspic does not set when the first layer is chilled, add about 1 tbsp gelatine and re-heat. Use as indicated in the recipe.

Time
Preparation takes about 45 minutes with about 4 hours chilling. Cooking takes about 4½ hours.

SERVES 6-8

CHRISTMAS BORSCH WITH PIEROZKI

Borsch was served at both Christmas and Easter celebrations
in Poland.

Dough
2 cups all-purpose flour
Pinch salt
5oz butter or margarine
1 egg
1 tbsp yogurt or sour cream

Filling
Mushroom from the borsch
1 tbsp butter or margarine
1 small onion, finely chopped
1-2 tbsps fresh breadcrumbs
1 small egg
Salt and pepper

Borsch
1 celeriac
3 parsley roots or 12 parsley stalks
4 carrots, peeled and roughly chopped
3 leeks
1 onion, thinly sliced
3lbs uncooked beets
10 black peppercorns
2 whole allspice berries
1 bay leaf
2-3oz dried mushrooms
Juice of 1-2 lemons
⅓ cup dry red wine
1 clove garlic, crushed

1. First prepare the Pierozki dough. Sift the flour with a pinch of salt into a large bowl. Cut the butter into small pieces and rub into the flour until the mixture resembles fine breadcrumbs.

2. Mix the egg and the yogurt or sour cream together and combine with the flour and butter to make a firm dough. Knead the dough together quickly into a bowl, wrap well and chill for 30 minutes.

3. Peel the celeriac root with a swivel vegetable peeler and chop the root roughly. Chop the parsley roots or slightly crush the stalks.

4. Cut the leeks in half lengthwise and rinse well under cold running water. Chop the leeks roughly and place all the vegetables, except beets, in a large stockpot. Add the black peppercorns, allspice berries and bay leaf and cover the vegetables with water. Cover and bring to the boil. Reduce the heat and allow to simmer, partially covered, for about 45 minutes.

5. Place the dried mushrooms in a small saucepan and cover with 2 cups water. Cover and bring to the boil. Allow to simmer until the mushrooms soften. Strain and add liquid to vegetable stock. Chop the mushrooms finely.

6. Melt 1 tbsp butter for the filling in a small pan and add the onion and chopped mushrooms. Cook briskly to evaporate moisture, and blend in the egg and bread-crumbs. Add enough crumbs to help the mixture hold its shape. Set the filling aside to cool completely. Roll out dough thinly on a well-floured surface. Cut into circles about 3 inches in diameter. Fill with a spoonful of filling, seal the edges with water and fold over to seal. Crimp with a fork, if desired. Bake on greased baking sheets in a pre-heated 425°F oven for about 10-15 minutes, or until brown and crisp.

7. After the vegetable stock has cooked 45 minutes, add peeled, grated beets, lemon juice, red wine and garlic, and cook a further 15-20 minutes, or until a good red color. Strain and serve immediately with the pierozki.

Cook's Notes

$ Buying Guide
Celeriac is a root vegetable with a strong taste of celery. If unavailable, substitute one head of celery, washed and roughly chopped. Include the celery leaves.

Variation
If dried mushrooms are unavailable, substitute 4oz fresh button mushrooms. Cook until the mushrooms are very soft.

Time
Preparation takes about 40 minutes, cooking takes about 1 hour.

SERVES 6-8

DUMPLING SOUP

Dumplings with a variety of fillings are very popular in Poland. Use fewer dumplings per serving for an appetizer, more for a filling soup.

6 cups home-made beef stock

Filling

6oz ground beef or pork
1 tsp chopped fresh marjoram
1 small onion, grated or very finely chopped
Salt and pepper

Dough

2 cups all-purpose flour, sifted
Pinch salt
1-2 eggs
4 tbsps water
Chopped parsley

1. Combine all the filling ingredients, mixing very well.

2. Prepare the dough by sifting the flour with a pinch of salt into a large bowl. Make a well in the centre and add the eggs and water. Use only one egg if they are large.

3. Using a wooden spoon, beat the ingredients together, gradually incorporating flour from the outside until the dough becomes too stiff to beat.

Step 3 If preparing dough by hand, use a wooden spoon to gradually incorporate the liquid and dry ingredients.

Step 5 Place a small spoonful of filling on top of each dough circle and brush the edges with water.

Step 6 Press together to seal well and crimp the edges with a fork if desired.

4. Knead the dough by hand until firm but elastic. Roll out the dough very thinly on a floured surface and cut into 3 inch rounds.

5. Place a small spoonful of filling on each dough circle and brush the edges with water.

6. Press the edges together to seal well, and crimp with a fork if desired.

7. Bring stock to the boil and add the dumplings. Cook about 10 minutes, or until all have floated to the surface.

8. Add parsley to the soup, adjust the seasoning and serve in individual bowls or from a large tureen.

Cook's Notes

Time
Home-made stock takes approximately 1 hour to cook. Dumplings take about 25 minutes to prepare and about 10 minutes to cook in the stock.

Serving Ideas
The dumplings may be cooked for the same length of time in water and dried and tossed with melted butter. Serve with sour cream and fresh dill or chives.

Variation
Chicken may be used in the dumpling filling in place of the beef or pork, and chicken stock substituted for beef stock.

SERVES 4-6

MUSHROOMS IN SOUR CREAM

This very old recipe originally called for freshly gathered forest mushrooms.

1lb button mushrooms, quartered
2 tbsps butter or margarine
6 green onions, thinly sliced
1 tbsp flour
1 tbsp lemon juice
2 tbsps chopped fresh dill or 1 tbsp dried dill
Pinch salt and pepper
⅓ cup sour cream
Paprika

1. Rinse the mushrooms and pat dry well. Trim the stalks level with the caps before quartering. Melt the butter in a sauté pan and add the mushrooms and onions. Sauté for about 1 minute and stir in the flour.

2. Add the lemon juice and all the remaining ingredients

Step 1 Sauté mushrooms and onions in the butter or margarine to soften.

Step 2 Add flour, lemon juice, herbs and seasoning and cook for 1 minute, stirring occasionally.

Step 3 Stir in the sour cream and heat through without boiling.

except the sour cream and paprika and cook slowly for about 1 minute.

3. Stir in the sour cream and adjust the seasoning. Heat through for about 1 minute. Spoon into individual serving dishes or on top of buttered toast. Sprinkle with paprika and serve immediately.

Cook's Notes

 Watchpoint
Sour cream will curdle if boiled, although the addition of flour to the sauce will help to stabilize it somewhat.

 Serving Ideas
Use as an appetizer or a side dish with meat, poultry or game. Prepare double quantity and serve with a salad and bread as a light lunch.

Time
Preparation takes about 20 minutes, cooking takes about 5-7 minutes.

SERVES 6

BEANS AND CARROTS POLISH STYLE

Breadcrumbs browned in butter are often
called a Polish sauce.

8oz green beans
8oz baby carrots with green tops
4 tbsps butter or margarine
4 tbsps dry breadcrumbs
½ tsp chopped fresh dill or marjoram
Salt and pepper

1. Top and tail the beans. This is easier done in several large bunches.

2. Leave some of the green tops on the carrots and peel them using a swivel vegetable peeler.

3. Place the carrots in cold salted water, cover the pan and bring to the boil. Cook for 10-15 minutes after the water comes to the boil. The beans may be added during the last 5 minutes of cooking time or they may be cooked separately.

Step 1 Top and tail the green beans. Gather them together in bunches and cut through with a sharp knife or trim off the ends with kitchen scissors.

Step 2 Cut off the green tops of the carrots, leaving a tiny amount of the stem, if desired. Peel with a swivel vegetable peeler or scrape with a small, sharp knife.

Step 4 Cook the breadcrumbs slowly in butter until golden brown. Stir frequently with a wooden spoon.

4. Melt the butter for the topping in a small saucepan and, when foaming, add the breadcrumbs, herbs, salt and pepper. Cook over low heat, stirring constantly until brown and crisp.

5. Drain the vegetables and mix them together. Sprinkle on the topping and serve.

Cook's Notes

 Time
Preparation takes about 20 minutes and cooking time a total of about 20 minutes.

 Preparation
The topping may be prepared ahead of time and tossed with the hot vegetables just before serving.

 Serving Ideas
Serve the vegetables as a side dish with meat, fish, poultry or game.

 Watchpoint
The breadcrumbs can burn easily so keep stirring them as they brown.

 Variation
Frozen vegetables may be used instead, and the cooking times altered according to package directions.

SERVES 6

NOODLES WITH POPPY SEEDS AND RAISINS

Christmas Eve dinner in Poland traditionally had up
to 21 courses, of which this was but one!

8oz noodles or other pasta shapes
Pinch salt
1 tbsp oil
½ cup heavy cream
6 tbsps black poppy seed, ground
2 tbsps honey
6 tbsps raisins

1. Bring lots of water to the boil in a large saucepan with a pinch of salt. Add the oil and the noodles or other pasta shapes and bring back to the boil. Cook, uncovered, until tender, about 10-12 minutes.

2. Drain and rinse the pasta under hot water. If using immediately, allow to drain dry. If not, place in a bowl of water to keep.

3. Place the cream in a deep, heavy-based saucepan and

Step 3 Cream is at scalding point when it begins to bubble round the edges. Remove quickly from heat, it can boil over.

Step 3 Pour the poppy seeds, honey and raisins into the cream, mixing very well.

Step 3 The poppy seed mixture should be thick when ready, but still fall from the spoon easily.

bring almost to the boil. When the cream reaches the scalding point, mix in the poppy seeds, honey and raisins. Cook slowly for about 5 minutes. The mixture should become thick but still fall off a spoon easily. Use a food processor or spice mill to grind the poppy seeds.

4. Toss the poppy seed mixture with the noodles and serve hot.

Cook's Notes

 Serving Ideas
Serve as a course on its own in a Polish Christmas Eve dinner or as a side dish to duck, pork or gammon.

 Time
Preparation takes about 15 minutes and cooking takes about 15-17 minutes.

 Variation
Use currants or golden raisins.

SERVES 4-6

CAULIFLOWER POLISH STYLE

A crunchy almond and golden fried breadcrumb topping
brightens up a plain boiled cauliflower.

1 large head cauliflower
4 tbsps butter or margarine
4 tbsps finely chopped blanched almonds
4 tbsps dry breadcrumbs
2 hard-boiled eggs
Chopped parsley and fresh dill

1. Remove the large coarse green leaves from the outside of the cauliflower. If desired, leave the fine pale green leaves attached.

2. Trim the stem and wash the cauliflower well.

3. Place the whole cauliflower in boiling water right side up. Add salt and bay leaf to the water and bring back to the boil. Cook the cauliflower for 12-15 minutes, or until just tender.

4. Melt the butter in a small frying pan and add the almonds. Cook slowly to brown. Stir in the breadcrumbs and cook about 1 minute or until crisp.

Step 1 Cut away the coarse green leaves with a sharp knife

Step 3 Place right side up in a pan of boiling water.

Step 4 Melt the butter in a small pan and add the almonds. Cook slowly to brown, stir in the breadcrumbs and cook for 1 minute, or until crisp.

5. Peel the eggs and cut them in half. Remove the yolks and cut the whites into thin strips. Press the yolks through a strainer.

6. When the cauliflower is cooked, drain it and place on serving dish. Spoon the breadcrumbs and almond topping over the cauliflower. Arrange the sliced egg white around the base of the cauliflower and sprinkle the egg yolks over the breadcrumb topping. Sprinkle over chopped parsley and dill. Serve immediately.

Cook's Notes

Time
Preparation takes about 20 minutes, cooking takes about 12-15 minutes.

Cook's Tip
Adding a bay leaf to the water when cooking cauliflower helps to neutralize the strong smell.

Watchpoint
Do not overcook cauliflower. It becomes watery very quickly.

SERVES 6

CUCUMBER SALAD

In Polish this salad is known by the name Mizeria
– quite a gloomy word for such a refreshing,
delicious and versatile salad and side dish.

1 large cucumber
½ cup sour cream
2 tsps white wine vinegar
1 tsp sugar
1 tbsp chopped fresh dill
Salt and pepper

1. Wash the cucumber well. Trim off the thin ends of the cucumber.

2. Using a cannelle knife or the prongs of a fork, score the skin of the cucumber in long strips.

3. Cut the cucumber into thin slices and place in a colander. Sprinkle with salt and leave for 30 minutes.

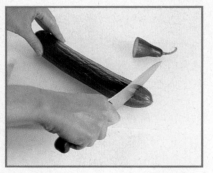

Step 1 Trim the ends of the cucumber so that the slices will all be even in size.

Step 2 Use a cannelle knife or a fork to make a decorative pattern in the skin of the cucumber.

Step 3 Sprinkle with salt. When the cucumber has been standing for 30 minutes, a lot of liquid will have been drawn out.

4. Place the colander in a bowl to collect the cucumber liquid. Rinse the cucumber well and pat dry.

5. Mix the remaining ingredients together in a large bowl and toss with the cucumber slices.

6. Arrange the cucumber in a serving dish and serve chilled.

Cook's Notes

 Preparation
Sprinkling cucumber lightly with salt and leaving it to stand will help draw out the moisture and keep the dressing from becoming watery. This also makes cucumbers easier to digest.

 Variation
Other chopped herbs may be used instead of, or in addition to, the dill.

Time
Preparation takes about 30 minutes.

SERVES 4-6

POLISH STYLE LETTUCE SALAD

Polish style in this case means the use of sour cream and hard-boiled egg in a dressing that really livens up plain lettuce salads.

1 head iceberg lettuce or 2 heads Webb or round lettuce
1 clove garlic
½ cup sour cream
Juice and grated rind of ½ lemon
½ tsp sugar
Salt and pepper
2 tsps chopped parsley
2 hard-boiled eggs

1. Break the lettuce into leaves and wash them well. Dry on paper towels or on a clean tea towel.

2. Peel a clove of garlic and crush it with the side of a large knife. Rub the clove of garlic on the inside of a salad bowl.

3. Tear the lettuce into bite-sized pieces and place in the salad bowl.

4. Mix together the remaining ingredients, except the

Step 2 Slightly crush the clove of garlic with the flat side of a knife or a fish slice.

Step 5 Chop the egg whites finely.

Step 6 Place egg yolks in a sieve and push through over a bowl.

hard-boiled eggs, and pour over the lettuce.

5. Cut the hard-boiled eggs in half, remove the yolks and chop the whites finely. Scatter the white over the top of the dressing.

6. Place the yolks in a small sieve and hold it over a bowl. Using the back of the spoon or your fingers, push the yolk through the holes in the sieve and sprinkle yolks over the salad. Serve immediately.

Cook's Notes

Cook's Tip
If hard-boiling eggs in advance, keep them submerged in cold water. This will prevent a gray ring from forming around the yolks.

Variation
Add other ingredients such as sliced cucumber, grated carrot or diced peppers to the salad.

Time
Preparation takes about 20 minutes. Hard-boiled eggs take about 9-10 minutes to cook.

SERVES 4

FRIED CARP

Carp is a favorite fish in Poland
and is prepared in numerous ways. This
dish is popular on Christmas Eve.

1 cleaned, filleted carp weighing about 2-3lbs
Salt
Flour
1-2 eggs, lightly beaten
Dry breadcrumbs
Butter and oil for frying

Cabbage and Mushrooms Polish Style

1lb canned sauerkraut
2-3oz dried mushrooms
2 tbsps butter or margarine
1 onion, thinly sliced or finely chopped
1½ tbsps flour
Salt and pepper

1. Cut the cleaned and scaled carp into even-sized portions and sprinkle lightly with salt. Leave to stand for half an hour. Skin, if desired.

2. Place the sauerkraut in a heavy-based saucepan and add 1 cup water. Bring to the boil and then allow to simmer until tender.

3. Place the mushrooms in a separate pan and add enough water to cover. Cook over gentle heat until softened. Slice the mushrooms and reserve them and their cooking liquid.

4. Melt the butter in a frying pan and, when foaming, add the onion. Cook in the butter until golden brown. Sprinkle

Step 8 Place crumbs on wax paper and lift the sides to toss the crumbs over the fish.

over the flour and mix thoroughly.

5. When the sauerkraut is tender, strain the cooking liquid over the butter mixture. Stir very well and bring to the boil. Cook until thickened and add to the sauerkraut, along with the sliced mushrooms and their liquid. Stir thoroughly and set aside to keep warm.

6. Dredge the carp lightly with flour, shaking off the excess.

7. Coat with beaten egg using a pastry brush, or dip the pieces into the egg using two forks.

8. Coat the fish with the crumbs, shaking off the excess. Heat the butter and oil together in a large frying pan until very hot. Place in the fish and cook on both sides until golden brown – about 5 minutes per side. Make sure the oil and butter come half way up the sides of the fish.

9. Drain fish on paper towels and serve immediately with the cabbage and mushrooms.

Cook's Notes

Time
Sauerkraut needs about 20-25 minutes to cook until tender. Fish will take about 10 minutes for both sides. It may be necessary to cook the fish in several batches, depending on the size of frying pan.

Preparation
To make coating the fillets easier, spread the crumbs out on a sheet of wax paper and place on a piece of fish coated with egg and lift the paper to toss the fillet from side to side to coat evenly.

Cook's Tip
After coating several pieces of fish, breadcrumbs may clump together with the egg. Sift the breadcrumbs through a strainer and discard the eggy bits.

SERVES 4

POLISH STYLE HERRING

Herring, prepared in any form, is a national
favorite in Poland. These fish can be prepared
well in advance and stored in their marinade.

4 even-sized herring, cleaned
2 onions, thinly sliced
10 black peppercorns
5 whole allspice berries
2 bay leaves
1 lemon, sliced
Juice of 3 lemons
½ cup cream
½ tsp sugar
4 potatoes, peeled and sliced
Salt, pepper and caraway seed
6 tbsps vegetable oil
Lemon wedges and chopped parsley to garnish

1. Place fish open end downward on a chopping board. Press along the backbone with the heel of your hand to loosen the bone.

2. Turn over and carefully pull out the main bone.

3. Cut the fillets in half and skin them using a filleting knife, beginning at the tail end and working up to the head end using a sawing motion, with the knife at an angle to the skin.

4. Layer up the fillets in a deep casserole, placing onion slices, spices, bay leaves and lemon slices between each layer.

5. Mix lemon juice and sugar together and pour over the fish. Place a sheet of wax paper directly over the top of the fish and cover with the casserole lid. Store in the refrigerator for 24 hours. Remove the fillets and strain the liquid. Mix 4

Step 2 Turn over and carefully pull out the bone.

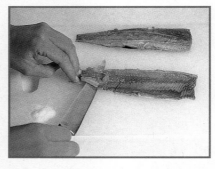

Step 3 Cut fillets in half and skin them using the same knife held at a slight angle. Dip fingers in salt to grip the fish skin more easily.

tbsps of the liquid with the cream and pour over the fillets to serve.

6. Layer the potatoes in an ovenproof serving dish and sprinkle salt, pepper, and caraway seeds in between each layer and on top. Spoon the oil over the top of the potatoes and bake, uncovered, in a preheated 400°F oven for about 30-40 minutes or until golden and cooked through. Serve with the herring. Garnish the dish with chopped parsley and lemon wedges.

Cook's Notes

Time
Herring takes about 25 minutes to prepare and must marinate in the refrigerator for 24 hours. Potatoes take about 15 minutes to prepare and 30-40 minutes to cook.

Preparation
To make the fish easier to skin, dip fingers in salt for a better grip on slippery skin.

Buying Guide
A fishmonger will clean and fillet the herrings for you if required.

SERVES 4-6

STUFFED FISH

A whole baked fish makes an impressive main course
for a dinner party. The stuffing makes the fish go
further and with no bones it's easy to serve and eat.

2-3lb whole fish such as carp, sea bass or salmon trout
2 tbsps melted butter

Stuffing

1 tbsp butter or margarine
1 small onion, finely chopped
4oz mushrooms, roughly chopped
1 hard-boiled egg, peeled and roughly chopped
¾ cup fresh breadcrumbs, white or whole-wheat
Pinch salt and pepper
2 tsps chopped fresh dill
2 tsps chopped fresh parsley
Pinch nutmeg

Sauce

½ cup sour cream
Pinch sugar
Grated rind and juice of ½ lemon
Pinch salt and white pepper
Lemon slices and parsley sprigs to garnish

1. Ask the fishmonger to gut and bone the fish for you, leaving on the head and tail. Sprinkle the cavity of the fish with salt and pepper and set it aside while preparing the stuffing.

2. To chop the onion finely, peel it and cut it in half lengthwise. Place the onion cut side down on a chopping board. Using a large, sharp knife, make four cuts into the onion, parallel to the chopping board, but not completely through to the root end. Using the pointed tip of the knife,

Step 2 Slice the onion crosswise into individual dice.

make four or five cuts into the onion lengthwise, following the natural lines in the onion and not cutting through to the root end. Next, cut the onion crossways into thin or thick slices as desired and the onion should fall apart into individual dice. Keep fingers well out of the way when slicing.

3. Melt the butter or margarine in a medium-sized saucepan and add the chopped onion and mushrooms. Cook briefly to soften the vegetables and set aside. Stir in the remaining stuffing ingredients.

4. Spread the stuffing evenly into the cavity of the fish and place the fish in lightly buttered foil or in a large baking dish. Sprinkle the top with melted butter and bake in a preheated 350°F oven for about 40 minutes, basting frequently. If the fish begins to dry out too much on top, cover loosely with aluminum foil.

5. When the fish is cooked, combine the sauce ingredients and pour over the fish. Cook a further 5 minutes to heat the sauce, but do not allow it to bubble. Remove the fish to a serving dish and garnish with lemon and parsley.

Cook's Notes

Cook's Tip
Cover the head and tail of the fish with lightly greased foil about halfway through cooking time. This will prevent the fish from drying out and improve the appearance of the finished dish.

Time
Preparation takes about 20 minutes. If boning the fish yourself, add a further 30 minutes. Cooking takes approximately 45 minutes.

Variation
Other vegetables, such as grated carrot, finely chopped green or red pepper or peeled, seeded and chopped tomatoes may be added to the stuffing.

SERVES 8-10

CABBAGE ROLLS

In Polish these are called Golabki, which translates
as 'little pigeons.' They make a tasty, inexpensive
supper dish, and you can improvise with different fillings.

1 head white cabbage or 2 heads green cabbage
6oz rice
4 tbsps butter or margarine
1 large onion, chopped
10oz ground pork, veal or beef
Salt and pepper
1 egg

Sauce

2 tbsps butter or margarine
2 tbsps flour
2lbs canned tomatoes
1 clove garlic, crushed
½ cup chicken stock
1 tsp chopped fresh thyme or ½ tsp dried thyme
Pinch sugar
Salt and pepper
2 tbsps tomato paste
4 tbsps chopped parsley

1. Cut the core out of the cabbage completely. Place cabbage in boiling salted water and cook for 15-20 minutes for green cabbage and 25-30 minutes for white cabbage. Remove and drain in a colander or on paper towels and leave to cool.

2. Cook the rice in boiling salted water for about 10 minutes or until almost tender. Drain and rinse under hot water to remove the starch. Leave in a colander and make five or six wells with the handle of a wooden spoon to allow the rice to drain thoroughly. Leave to dry.

3. Melt 4 tbsps butter or margarine in a large frying pan and cook the onion for about 3 minutes, or until slightly softened. Add the meat and cook slowly just until the meat

Step 5 Fold in
the sides around
the filling and
then roll up the
leaves from the
thick end to the
thin end.

loses its pink color. Break the meat up with a fork as it cooks. Add salt, pepper, rice and egg and set aside to cool.

4. Separate the cabbage leaves and trim down the spines with a small, sharp knife. Place all the leaves out on a clean work surface and divide the filling evenly among all the leaves.

5. To roll up, fold in the sides around the filling and roll up from the thick end to the thin end.

6. Place all the cabbage rolls in a tightly fitting casserole. It may be necessary to have two layers of rolls and possibly three. Pour water into the casserole to come about half way up the rolls. Cover the casserole tightly and cook in a pre-heated 375°F oven for 30 minutes.

7. To prepare the sauce, put 2 tbsps butter or margarine in a heavy-based pan and stir in the flour. Cook for 1-2 minutes and add all the remaining ingredients except the chopped parsley. Bring to the boil, stirring continuously. Partially cover the pan and cook for 20 minutes over low heat. Break up the tomatoes with a fork as the sauce cooks.

8. Check the level of liquid in the casserole. Pour away all but ½ cup. Pour on the tomato sauce and cook, uncovered, for a further 20 minutes, or until the cabbage is tender. Sprinkle with chopped parsley before serving.

Cook's Notes

Time
Preparation takes about 30 minutes, cooking takes about 15-20 minutes to pre-cook the cabbage and 50 minutes to cook the cabbage rolls.

Variation
Substitute mushrooms for the meat in the recipe or add chopped, cooked ham and chopped hard-boiled eggs.

Preparation
Trimming the spines of the cabbage leaves makes them easier to roll up.

SERVES 6

STUFFED ROAST BEEF

The roasting is done on top of the stove instead
of in the oven. This means a succulent piece
of meat with a moist stuffing.

2lb beef joint
Flour
1 cup beef stock
1 bay leaf
1 blade mace

Stuffing

4 tbsps butter or margarine
3 medium onions, peeled and finely chopped
3-4 slices bread, made into crumbs
Grated rind and juice of ½ lemon
2 tsps chopped parsley
1 tsp chopped thyme
1 egg
Pinch paprika
Salt and pepper

Step 6 Spread
the stuffing
between each
slice.

Step 6 Press the
joint back into
shape and return
to the pan.

1. Melt half of the butter in a large saucepan. Coat the meat with flour and brown the meat in the butter on all sides.

2. Pour the stock into the casserole and add the bay leaf, blade mace and a pinch of pepper. Cover the pan and cook on top of the stove over low heat for about 45 minutes, turning the joint from time to time and adding more water or stock if necessary.

3. Remove the joint from the casserole and place it on a cutting board to stand for 10-15 minutes.

4. Melt the remaining butter in a saucepan and add the chopped onions. Cook until the onions are tender, but not brown. Add the breadcrumbs and remaining stuffing in-gredients, beating well to mix thoroughly.

5. Slice the joint thinly, but without cutting completely through the meat.

6. Spread an even amount of stuffing between each slice of meat and press the joint back into shape. Return the joint to the casserole for a further 35-40 minutes. When the meat is tender, remove it to a serving dish and boil the pan juices rapidly until of syrupy consistency. Pour some over the joint and serve the rest separately.

Cook's Notes

Time
Preparation takes about 30 minutes, and cooking time about 1 hour 15 minutes.

Variation
If rare roast beef is desired, cook for only 20 minutes after stuffing.

Serving Ideas
Serve with mashed potatoes and red cabbage.

SERVES 8

HUNTER'S STEW

The tradition of this stew − bigos in Polish − goes back centuries. It was kept in supplies in well-stocked larders, taken on long road journeys and eaten on feast days.

4 tbsps oil
¾lb stewing steak, pork or venison cut in 2 inch pieces
1 onion
2 cloves garlic, crushed
4 tbsps flour
2 tbsps mild paprika
4 cups light stock
4oz smoked ham, cut in 2 inch pieces
4oz smoked sausage, cut in 2 inch pieces
1 tsp marjoram
1 tsp chopped thyme
1 tsp chopped parsley
Salt and pepper
Pinch cayenne pepper (optional)
2 tbsps tomato paste
1 head white cabbage, chopped
2 apples, cored and chopped
2 carrots, thinly sliced
8 pitted prunes, roughly chopped
3 tomatoes, peeled and roughly chopped
⅓ cup red wine or Madeira
Pinch sugar (optional)

1. Heat the oil in a large, flameproof casserole. Slice onion thickly and add with the garlic and cook 2-3 minutes. Remove and set aside.

2. Add the meat in four small batches, cooking over high heat to brown.

3. When all the meat is browned, return it to the casserole with the onions and garlic. Sprinkle over the flour and cook until light brown.

Step 1 To slice an onion, peel and cut in half. Leave the root end on to hold the onion together and place cut side down on a chopping board.

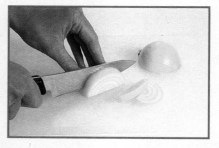

Step 1 Using a large, sharp knife, slice the onion, keeping the fingers out of the way. Alternatively, hold with a fork.

4. Add paprika and cook 1-2 minutes, stirring constantly.

5. Pour on the stock gradually and bring to the boil. Turn down the heat to simmering and add the smoked meats, herbs, salt, pepper, cayenne and tomato purée.

6. Stir well, cover and cook over low heat for 45 minutes. Stir occasionally and add more liquid if necessary during cooking.

7. When the meat is almost tender, add cabbage, apples, carrots and prunes. Cook a further 20 minutes.

8. Add the tomatoes, wine or Madeira and a pinch of sugar, if desired. Cook a further 10 minutes, adjust the seasoning and serve immediately.

Cook's Notes

Time
Preparation takes about 25 minutes and cooking takes about 1 hour 25 minutes in total.

Serving Ideas
Accompany with rice, mashed potatoes or bread. The stew may be eaten hot or cold.

Variation
Use a combination of beef, pork and venison if desired.

SERVES 4

FILLED BEEF ROLLS

Zrazy, thin slices of tender beef, go back to the 14th century in Polish cuisine. There are different kinds of zrazy and many different stuffings for the rolled variety.

8 thin frying steaks, trimmed
2 dill pickles, cut in thin strips
4oz cooked ham steak, cut in thin strips
2 green onions, shredded
Mustard
4 tbsps oil
2 tbsps flour
1 cup beef stock
4 tbsps white wine
1 tbsp tomato paste
Salt and pepper
4 tbsps sour cream or thick yogurt
Chopped parsley

Step 4 Divide the filling ingredients among all the pieces of meat and fold in the sides.

Step 4 Roll the ends of the meat over the filling to cover completely and secure with string or wooden picks.

1. Place each steak between two sheets of damp wax paper and bat out with a meat mallet or rolling pin to flatten.

2. Cut the dill pickles, ham and green onions into even-sized lengths.

3. Spread the meat thinly with the mustard and divide the dill pickles, ham and onions among all the slices.

4. Fold in the sides of the meat about ½ inch. Roll the meat around the filling and secure with wooden picks or tie with fine string.

5. Heat the oil in a large sauté pan and when hot, brown the beef rolls. It may be necessary to brown them in two batches. Remove the meat and set aside.

6. Add the flour to the pan and allow to cook until light

brown. Gradually stir in the stock and add the wine, tomato paste, salt and pepper. Bring to the boil and allow to simmer for one minute.

7. Return the beef rolls to the pan and spoon over some of the sauce. Cover and cook over low heat for 45 minutes to 1 hour. Add more liquid as necessary during cooking.

8. When the beef rolls are cooked, transfer them to a serving dish and remove the wooden picks or string. Spoon over the sauce and top with the sour cream and chopped parsley to serve.

Cook's Notes

Variation
Other filling ingredients such as mushrooms, sauerkraut, herbs and breadcrumbs or horse-radish and breadcrumbs bound with egg may be used.

Time
Preparation takes about 25 minutes, cooking takes about 1 hour.

Serving Ideas
Serve with pasta, rice or mashed potatoes.

SERVES 6-8

ROAST PORK IN WILD GAME STYLE

The love of game is part of Polish culinary history, so even meat from domestic animals was often given the same treatment.

3lb boneless pork roast
Paprika
4 tbsps lard or dripping
¾ cup sour cream or thick yogurt
1 tsp flour
1 tbsp chopped fresh dill

Marinade

1 carrot, finely chopped
2 celery sticks, finely chopped
1 bay leaf
5 black peppercorns
5 allspice berries
2 sprigs thyme
10 juniper berries, slightly crushed
2 onions, sliced
½ cup dry white wine
Juice and grated rind of 1 lemon

Beet Accompaniment

4 tbsps butter or margarine
2 tbsps flour
1 onion, finely chopped
1 clove garlic, crushed
½ cup chicken or vegetable stock
2lbs cooked beet, peeled and grated or cut into small dice
White wine vinegar
Sugar, salt and pepper

Step 2 Heat the fat in a roasting pan and brown the pork joint on all sides in the hot fat.

1. First combine the marinade ingredients in a small saucepan and bring to the boil. Allow to cool. Place the pork in a casserole dish or bowl and pour over the marinade. Cover and refrigerate for two days, turning the meat frequently. Remove the meat from the marinade and wipe it dry with paper towels. Reserve the marinade.

2. Heat the lard or dripping in a roasting pan. Sprinkle the fat side of the pork with paprika, and brown the pork on all sides in the hot fat. Pour over marinade after one hour's cooking. Cook, uncovered, in a preheated 375°F oven for 2 hours and 15 minutes. Baste frequently with the pan juices.

3. Remove the pork from the pan and set aside. Skim any fat from the surface of the sauce and strain the vegetables and meat juices into a saucepan. Mix the flour, sour cream, and dill together and add to the pan. Bring just to the boil, turn down the heat and allow to simmer for 1-2 minutes.

4. Grate the beet or cut it into small dice. Melt the butter in a heavy-based saucepan and add the flour and onion. Stir well and cook over moderate heat until light brown. Add the garlic and stir in the stock gradually.

5. Bring to the boil, add beet, sugar, vinegar, salt and pepper to taste and cook for ten minutes over moderate heat. Stir occasionally to prevent sticking.

6. To serve, slice the pork and pour over the sauce. Serve with the beet. Crackling can be removed and sliced separately to make carving easier.

Cook's Notes

Time
The beet takes approximately 10 minutes to cook. The pork should be roasted for 30 minutes to the pound and 30 minutes over.

Watchpoint
Beet will lose its color if overcooked or reheated. Make the beet accompaniment just before serving.

SERVES 6

ROAST PORK WITH CARAWAY SEEDS

In old Poland, pork was the most popular meat because there was such an abundance of wild boar in the forests.

2lb pork roast
Salt
Marjoram
2 tsps caraway seed
1½ tbsps lard or oil
2 onions, sliced
1 cup stock

Potato Kopytka

2lbs potatoes, peeled and cooked
1 large egg
1lb all-purpose flour
Salt

Step 2 Score the fat in a chequerboard pattern, and sprinkle with salt, marjoram and caraway seeds.

1. Remove the crackling, leaving most of the fat on the joint. Place crackling in a shallow pan, brush lightly with oil and sprinkle with salt.

2. Score the fat of the joint in a checkerboard pattern. Sprinkle with salt, a pinch of marjoram and the caraway seeds at least one hour before cooking.

3. Heat the lard in a roasting pan and brown the meat, fat side down first. Cook on all sides and then turn over fat side down again. Add the onions and the stock.

4. Roast in a preheated 425°F oven for 30 minutes. Turn over and continue roasting for 45 minutes or until the juices run clear, basting frequently with the cooking liquid. Cook the crackling at the same time, turning it over halfway through the cooking time.

5. Meanwhile, cook the potatoes, drain them, place back

in the pan and toss over high heat to dry completely. Push them through a sieve into a large bowl. Beat in the egg and gradually add the flour with a good pinch of salt. It may not be necessary to add all the flour, but the mixture should be very stiff.

6. Turn the mixture out onto a floured surface and knead until a smooth dough forms.

7. Divide the dough into 4-6 pieces and roll each into a sausage shape about 1 inch thick. Cut into diagonal pieces about 2 inches long.

8. Drop the dough pieces into boiling salted water and cook until they float to the surface and are slightly firm.

9. Drain the dumplings and keep warm. Carve the joint into slices or bring to the table whole. Skim the fat from the surface of the pan juices and reduce them slightly if necessary by boiling over high heat. Pour around the meat to serve.

10. Crumble the crackling over the Kopytka and serve with the pork.

Cook's Notes

 Variation
Serve Kopytka with butter instead of crackling. They may be served with other roast meats, poultry or game.

Time
Preparation takes about 35-40 minutes, cooking takes about 1 hour 15 minutes.

 Serving Ideas
Add a green vegetable or serve with cucumber salad.

SERVES 2

Roast Pigeon with Juniper Sauce

This sauce goes as well with
venison as it does with game birds.

2 pigeons, dressed
4oz chicken liver pâté
1 tbsp brandy
6 strips bacon

Sauce

2oz smoked bacon, chopped
1 onion, finely chopped
½ carrot, finely chopped
1 stick celery, finely chopped
1 tbsp juniper berries
2 tbsps flour
1 cup stock
½ cup white wine
1 tsp tomato paste (optional)
Salt and pepper

Step 1 Remove pin feathers with tweezers or singe the pigeons over an open flame.

Step 5 Cook the vegetables and juniper berries in the bacon fat until they begin to brown lightly.

1. Pluck any pin feathers from the pigeons with tweezers or singe them over a gas flame.

2. Mix pâté and brandy together and spread on the insides of each pigeon.

3. Tie the bacon on the pigeons to cover the breasts and roast them in a preheated 400°F oven for 35-40 minutes.

4. Meanwhile, place chopped bacon in a heavy-based saucepan over low heat. Cook slowly to render the fat.

5. Add the vegetables and juniper berries and cook until the vegetables begin to brown lightly.

6. Add the flour and cook until golden brown.

7. Pour on stock gradually, stirring continuously. Bring to the boil and reduce the heat to simmer. Partially cover the pan and cook slowly for about 20-25 minutes. Add more stock or water as necessary.

8. Skim the fat from the roasting pan and discard it. Add pan juices to the sauce and pour in the juices from the cavity of each pigeon.

9. Strain the sauce into a clean pan and add the wine and tomato paste, if using.

10. Bring to the boil for about 3 minutes to reduce slightly. Season with salt and pepper and serve with the pigeons.

Cook's Notes

Variation
Use pheasant when in season. Hen pheasants are more tender than cock pheasants. If using cock pheasants, increase the cooking time to 40-50 minutes.

Serving Ideas
Accompany with noodles or potatoes. Serving and eating are easier if the pigeons are cut in half first.

Watchpoint
Do not allow the vegetables to get too brown before adding the flour or the sauce will taste bitter.

SERVES 4

CHICKEN POLISH STYLE

Choose small, young chickens for a truly Polish
style dish. A dried white roll was originally
used for stuffing, but breadcrumbs are easier.

2 chickens, weighing approximately 2lbs each
2 chicken livers
1 tbsp butter or margarine
6 slices bread, made into crumbs
2 tsps chopped parsley
1 tsp chopped dill
1 egg
Salt and pepper
½ cup chicken stock

1. Remove the fat from just inside the cavities of the chickens and discard it. Melt the butter in a small frying pan. Pick over the chicken livers and cut away any discolored portions. Add chicken livers to the butter and cook until just brown. Chop and set aside.

2. Combine the breadcrumbs, egg, herbs, salt and pepper and mix well. Mix in the chopped chicken livers.

3. Stuff the cavities of the chickens and sew up the openings. Tie the legs together.

4. Place the chickens in a roasting pan and spread the breasts and legs lightly with more butter. Pour the stock

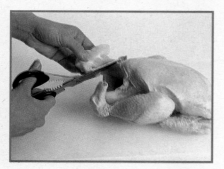

Step 1 Remove the fat from the inside of the cavity of each chicken and discard it.

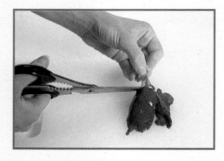

Step 1 Pick over the chicken livers and remove any discolored parts.

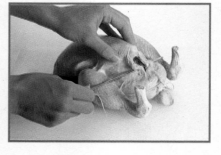

Step 3 Fill the chickens and sew up the opening with fine thread using a trussing needle.

around the chickens and roast in a preheated 375°F oven for about 40-45 minutes. Baste frequently with the pan juices during roasting.

5. To check if the chickens are done, pierce the thickest part of the thigh with a skewer or small, sharp knife. If the juices run clear the chickens are ready. If the juices are pink, return to the oven for another 5-10 minutes.

6. When the chickens are done, remove them from the roasting pan, remove the strings and keep them warm. Skim any fat from the surface of the pan juices. If a lot of liquid has accumulated, pour into a small saucepan and reduce over high heat. Pour the juices over the chicken to serve.

Cook's Notes

 Serving Ideas
Serve with a cucumber salad or a Polish style lettuce salad and new potatoes tossed with butter and dill.

 Variation
Chopped mushrooms or onions may be added to the stuffing, if desired.

 Time
Preparation takes about 20 minutes and cooking takes about 45 minutes.

SERVES 2-3

DUCK IN CAPER SAUCE

A sweet-sour sauce with the tang of
capers is a perfect accompaniment to
a rich meat such as duck.

4½lb whole duck, giblets removed
1 clove garlic, crushed
Salt and pepper
1 tbsp oil
3 tbsps butter or margarine
1 cup chicken stock
4 tbsps sugar
½ cup water
1 tbsp vinegar or lemon juice
6 tbsps capers
4 tsps cornstarch mixed with 2 tbsps water

1. Rub the cavity of the duck with the crushed garlic and sprinkle in salt and pepper. Leave to stand 1-2 hours but do not refrigerate.

2. Heat the oil in a heavy frying pan or roasting pan and when hot add the butter or margarine. Prick the duck skin all over with a sharp fork and brown the duck on all sides in the butter or oil. Transfer the duck to a saucepan or flameproof casserole.

3. Pour over the stock, cover and simmer over medium heat for about 1 hour 40 minutes, or until the duck is tender.

4. Meanwhile, heat the water and sugar together slowly in a small, heavy-based saucepan until the sugar dissolves.

5. Once the sugar is dissolved, turn up the heat and allow the syrup to boil rapidly until it caramelizes. Remove from the heat and pour in the vinegar or lemon juice. It will splutter. Add several spoonfuls of the cooking liquid from the duck and set the caramel over medium heat. Allow mixture to come to the boil, stirring constantly.

Step 2 Brown the duck in a mixture of oil and butter over brisk heat.

Step 4 Combine the sugar and the water in a heavy-based saucepan and cook to dissolve the sugar and make a clear syrup.

6. When the duck is tender, remove it to a heated serving dish. Skim off the fat from the cooking liquid and discard. Mix the water and cornstarch together and add several spoonfuls of the duck cooking liquid. Return to the rest of the liquid and bring to the boil. Add the capers and stir over high heat until the sauce clears and thickens. Add the caramel and stir until the sauce is thick.

7. Cut the duck into portions or serve whole and spoon over some of the sauce. Serve the rest of the sauce separately.

Cook's Notes

Cook's Tip
Pricking the duck skin with a sharp fork allows the fat to run out as the duck cooks. Use this method when roasting or pot roasting to produce duck that is not fatty.

Watchpoint
Keep a close eye on the caramel as it browns. It can burn very quickly. Use an oven glove when adding the vinegar or hot liquid to the caramel as it will splutter.

Time
Preparation takes about 20 minutes with 1-2 hours standing time for the duck. Cooking takes about 1 hour.

SERVES 4
ROAST QUAIL

Quail are delicate, very elegant birds that are
perfect as a dinner party dish. They are also easy to
prepare and quick to cook – a bonus when entertaining.

8 dressed quail
8 thin slices pork fat or 8 strips bacon
Fresh sage leaves
4oz butter
8 slices white bread, crusts removed
Whole cranberry sauce or blueberry preserves with the
　　juice of ½ lemon

1. Remove any pin feathers from the birds and wash them
under cold running water. Dry thoroughly inside and out.
Salt lightly inside and place a fresh sage leaf inside each
quail.

2. Tie the pork fat or bacon strips around each bird.

3. Melt the butter over a low heat and brush over each bird
before placing them in a preheated 400°F oven for about
20-25 minutes. Baste the quail from time to time with the
melted butter and the pan juices.

Step 2 Using fine
string, tie the pork
fat or bacon strips
around each
quail.

Step 4 Cut the
slices of bread
about the same
size as the quails.
Cut in rectangles
or ovals with a
pastry cutter.

Step 4 Cook the
bread in melted
butter until nicely
browned on both
sides.

4. Put the remaining butter in a large frying pan and place
over fairly high heat. When hot, add slices of bread which
have been cut to a size to fit the quail. Brown them on both
sides in the butter and remove to paper towels to drain.

5. When the quail are cooked, remove the threads and
take off the bacon or pork fat, if desired. The fat or bacon
may be served with the quail. Place each quail on a piece of
fried bread and serve with whole cranberry sauce or the
blueberry preserves mixed with the lemon juice. Spoon
some of the pan juices over each quail before serving.

Cook's Notes

Variation
Frozen quail may be used in
place of fresh quail. Allow to
defrost completely before roasting. If
neither are available, use pigeons or
poussins and increase the cooking
time to 35-40 minutes.

Time
Preparation takes about 20-25
minutes and cooking takes
about 20 minutes.

Serving Ideas
Serve with new potatoes and
fresh peas.

SERVES 8

SWEET PIEROZKI

In Polish cuisine, dumplings can be sweet as well
as savory. Surprisingly, these are often eaten as
a side dish to meat or as a main dish by themselves.

Dough

Full quantity dough recipe for Christmas Borsch with
    Pierozki
Oil for Frying

Cheese Filling

8oz dry cottage cheese
1 egg yolk
2 tbsps sugar
2 tsps finely chopped candied orange peel
2 tbsps currants

Plum Filling

4-6 purple plums, halved, stoned and chopped
1/3 cup sugar
Sour cream
Grated nutmeg or cinnamon

1. Prepare the dough as for the Pierozki in the Christmas
Borsch recipe. Roll out very thinly on a well-floured surface
and cut into circles about 3 inches in diameter.

2. For the cheese filling, beat the cottage cheese, egg yolk
and sugar together until smooth. Stir in the peel and the
currants by hand. Place a spoonful of the filling on half of the

Step 2 Place the
dough circles out
on a clean sur-
face. Fill half with
cheese and half
with plums.

Step 4 Drop the
filled and sealed
pierozki into
boiling water and
cook until they
float to the
surface.

Step 5 Cook the
drained pierozki in
oil until lightly
browned on both
sides.

dough circles and moisten the edges with water. Fold over
the top and seal the edges well, crimping with a fork if
desired.

3. On the remaining half of the dough circles, place on
some of the chopped plums and sprinkle with sugar. Seal
the edges as before.

4. To cook the Pierozki, drop a few at a time into boiling
water. Simmer for 2-3 minutes or until they float to the top. Lift
out of the water with a slotted spoon and drain on paper
towels.

5. When all the Pierozki are done, heat about 4 tbsps oil in
a frying pan and cook the Pierozki over brisk heat for about
3-4 minutes, or until lightly browned on both sides. Place
the Pierozki on a serving plate and top with sour cream
sprinkled with nutmeg or cinnamon.

Cook's Notes

Time
Preparation takes about 50-60
minutes, cooking takes about
2-3 minutes per batch of Pierozki and
3-4 minutes for frying.

Variation
Other fruit such as pitted
cherries, apricots or peaches,
stoned and chopped, may be used.

Preparation
Pierozki can be cooked in
advance and fried just before
serving.

MAKES 2 ROLLS

POPPY SEED CAKE

This is the Christmas version of an ever popular
Polish cake. As a symbol of holiday generosity, more
poppy seeds were used than in the everyday recipe.

Pastry Dough

6 cups all-purpose flour
¾ cup sugar
1½ sticks butter or margarine
2 eggs
⅓-½ cup milk
3 tbsps yeast
Pinch salt

Filling

8oz poppy seeds
1½ cups milk
⅓ cup butter or margarine
½ cup honey
4 tbsps ground walnuts
3oz raisins
2 tbsps finely chopped candied peel
2 eggs
½ cup sugar
⅓ cup brandy

1. To prepare the dough, cream the butter with the sugar until light and fluffy and gradually add the eggs, beating well in between each addition. Add a pinch of salt and heat the milk until lukewarm. Dissolve the yeast in the milk and add to the other ingredients. Sift in the flour and knead the dough until smooth and elastic.

2. When kneading dough, be sure to stretch it well and work on a lightly-floured surface. If necessary, flour hands if the dough tends to stick.

3. To test if the dough has been sufficiently kneaded, press lightly with two fingers. If the dough springs back fairly quickly, it is ready to leave to rise.

Step 8 Roll up the dough as for a jelly roll.

4. Place the dough in a lightly greased bowl, cover with a cloth or lightly greased plastic wrap and leave for about 1 hour, or until doubled in bulk. Keep in a warm place.

5. Bring the milk for the filling to the boil and mix with the poppy seeds. Cook over low heat for about 30 minutes, stirring frequently. Drain the poppy seed well and blend to a paste in a food processor or liquidizer.

6. Melt the butter and add the honey, walnuts, raisins and peel. Add the poppy seed and cook for about 15 minutes, stirring frequently over moderate heat.

7. Beat the eggs with the sugar until light and fluffy and combine with the poppy seed mixture. Cook over gentle heat, stirring constantly to thicken. Add the brandy and set the filling aside.

8. When the dough has doubled in bulk, knock it back and knead for a further 2-5 minutes. Divide dough in half. Roll each half out thinly on a floured surface, shaping into rectangles. Spread the filling evenly over each piece and roll up as for a jelly roll. Roll up tightly, pressing the ends together to seal. Place on a lightly buttered baking sheet curving into a horse shoe. Bake in a preheated 375°F oven for 45-50 minutes, or until golden brown. Serve with or without icing.

Cook's Notes

! Watchpoint
Do not mix the yeast into milk that is too hot. This can kill the yeast and the dough will not rise as it should.

 Variation
1 tsp almond or vanilla extract may be used instead of the brandy.

 Time
Preparation takes about 1 hour, cooking takes about 45-50 minutes.

MAKES 36

CRULLERS

These are crisp, light biscuits that are fried
like fritters. They are best eaten on the day they
are made and are lovely with coffee or tea.

2 egg yolks
1 whole egg
4 tbsps sugar
4 tbsps whipping cream
1¼ cups all-purpose flour
Pinch salt
Powdered sugar
Oil for deep frying

Step 5 Cut slits in
the lower half of
each strip.

Step 6 Pull one
end of each strip
through the slit
before frying in
hot oil.

1. Beat yolks and whole egg together until thick and lemon colored, about 10 minutes. Add the sugar and beat well to dissolve. Sift the flour with a pinch of salt and whisk half of it into the egg mixture, alternating with the cream. Fold in the remaining flour. Leave to stand 30 minutes in a cool place.

2. Turn the dough out onto a well-floured surface and knead with floured hands. Dough will be sticky at first.

3. Roll out until very thin with a well-floured rolling pin on a well-floured surface.

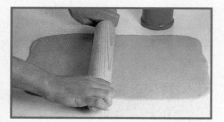

Step 4 Roll out
dough paper thin
and cut strips with
a pastry wheel.

4. Using a fluted pastry wheel, cut into strips about 3x1½ inches.

5. Cut a slit in the lower half of each piece.

6. Pull one end through the slit. Deep fry at 350°F until golden brown on both sides, about 3-4 minutes. Drain on paper towels and sprinkle with powdered sugar before serving.

Cook's Notes

Time
Preparation takes about 45 minutes and cooking takes about 3-4 minutes per batch.

Serving
Serve as an accompaniment to fruit or ice cream, or serve with coffee or tea.

Preparation
Cook a maximum of 6 crullers at a time.

SERVES 8

ROYAL MAZUREK

Mazureks are flat pastry cakes and there are many
different recipes for these. The dough needs careful
handling, but the result is well worth the effort.

1½ sticks butter or margarine
4 tbsps sugar
6 tbsps blanched almonds, finely chopped
½ tsp grated lemon rind
2½ cups all-purpose flour
Yolks of 2 hard-boiled eggs, sieved
1 raw egg yolk
Pinch salt
Pinch cinnamon
Apricot and raspberry or cherry preserves
Powdered sugar

1. Cream the butter and the sugar together until light and
fluffy. Stir in the almonds, lemon rind, flour and egg yolks by
hand. Add the egg yolk and a pinch of salt and cinnamon,
and mix all the ingredients into a smooth dough. This may
be done in a food processor. Wrap well and leave in the
refrigerator for about 1 hour.

2. Roll out ⅔ of the dough and place on a baking sheet. If
dough cracks, press back into place. Keep remaining ⅓ of
the dough in the refrigerator.

Step 1 Cream the
butter and sugar
together until light
and fluffy

Step 2 Roll out
the dough on a
well-floured sur-
face with a well-
floured rolling pin.
Alternatively, roll
directly onto the
baking sheet.

Step 3 Arrange
the strips in a
latticework pattern
on top of the
pastry base,
pressing edges
together well.

3. Roll out the remaining dough and cut into thin strips
about ¼ inch thick. Arrange these strips on top of the
dough in a lattice pattern and press the edges to seal.

4. Brush the pastry with a mixture of 1 beaten egg with a
pinch of salt. Bake in a preheated 375°F oven for about
20-30 minutes, or until light golden brown and crisp.
Loosen the pastry from the baking sheet but do not remove
until completely cool. Place the pastry on a serving plate
and spoon some of the preserves into each of the open
spaces of the lattice work. Alternate the two flavors of
preserves. Sprinkle lightly with powdered sugar before
serving.

Cook's Notes

Time
Preparation takes about 30
minutes with 1 hour chilling for
the pastry. Cooking takes about 20-30
minutes.

Variation
Use other finely chopped nuts
in the pastry and other
varieties of preserves.

Cook's Tip
If lattice strips break, press
ends together and they will
stick together again.

MAKES 2 CAKES

SAFFRON BABAS

This is a traditional Easter cake. Cooks spoke in
whispers when these cakes were cooling since loud
noise was believed to damage the delicate texture!

2½ cups all-purpose flour
1½ cups lukewarm milk
3 envelopes dry yeast
¾ cup sugar
8 egg yolks
4 egg whites
Rind of 1 lemon
3 tbsps brandy
Pinch saffron powder
7½ cups all-purpose flour
Pinch salt
1½ sticks melted butter, slightly cooled
1 cup golden raisins
2 tbsps candied peel

1. First prepare a batter with 2½ cups flour. Combine the
milk and yeast and pour into a well in the center of the flour.
Mix with a wooden spoon and cover the bowl.

2. Leave in a warm place for about 1 hour, covered with a
cloth or plastic wrap, until it doubles in bulk and the top
becomes bubbly.

3. Combine the sugar together with the egg yolks, egg
whites, lemon rind, brandy and saffron. Mix with the yeast
mixture and add the remaining flour and salt. Knead the

Step 1 Sift the
flour into a bowl
and make a well
in the center. Pour
in the milk and
yeast mixture and
stir to form a
dough.

Step 2 Leave in a
warm place until
doubled in bulk
and bubbly on
top.

Step 4 Leave the
dough to rise a
second time in
the baking dish
until it is filling it
completely.

dough by hand for about 30 minutes in the bowl or on a very
well-floured surface.

4. Place the dough back in the bowl and add the butter,
raisins and peel. Knead the dough by hand until it is smooth
and elastic and does not stick. Divide in 2 equal portions.
Butter 2 10 inch round cake pans very thickly and place in
the dough, patting out evenly. Cover with lightly-oiled
plastic wrap and put in a warm place to rise until it fills the
pan. Bake in a pre-heated 400°F oven for about 60 minutes.

5. Test with a metal skewer. If the skewer comes out clean
when inserted into the center of the babas the cakes are
done. Leave to cool in the pans for about 10-14 minutes and
then remove to a cooling rack. Sprinkle with sugar or drizzle
with icing.

Cook's Notes

! Watchpoint
Do not mix the yeast with milk
that is too hot. This can kill the
yeast and the cakes will not rise as they
should.

 Time
Preparation takes about
2 hours, cooking takes about
1 hour.

SERVES 6-8

BUCKWHEAT AND RAISIN PUDDING

Of all the cereals or kashas used in Polish cooking,
buckwheat was the most highly prized.

3 cups milk
1 vanilla pod
6 tbsps butter or margarine
1 cup buckwheat
4 eggs, separated
¾ cup sugar
1-1¼ cups raisins
Grated rind of half a lemon
Red cherry preserves

1. Boil the milk with the vanilla pod in a large saucepan.

2. Stir in 4 tbsps of the butter until melted. Reserve remaining butter.

3. Pick over the buckwheat and add it to the milk, stirring well.

4. Cook, uncovered, over low heat, stirring occasionally to prevent sticking.

5. When the mixture thickens, transfer it to an ovenproof dish with a tight fitting lid. Bake in a preheated 375°F oven for 45 minutes. Remove the vanilla pod and allow the

Step 2 Boil milk with the vanilla pod in a large saucepan and stir in 4 tbsps of the butter.

Step 6 Beat the egg yolks with the sugar until light and fluffy.

Step 7 Whisk the egg whites just until stiff peaks form.

mixture to cool slightly.

6. Beat the egg yolks with the sugar until light and fluffy. Add lemon rind, mix with the buckwheat, and stir in the raisins.

7. Whisk egg whites until stiff peaks form and fold into the buckwheat mixture.

8. Smooth the top of the pudding and dot with the remaining butter. Bake a further 30 minutes at 375°F.

9. Serve topped with cherry preserves and cream, if desired.

Cook's Notes

Variation
Substitute golden raisins, currants or mixed peel for the raisins if desired.

Cook's Tip
Vanilla pods and cinnamon sticks may be used several times. Rinse and dry after use and store air tight.

Time
Preparation takes about 20 minutes, cooking takes a total of 1 hour 25 minutes.

INDEX

ACKNOWLEDGMENT
The publishers wish to thank the following suppliers
for their kind assistance:
Corning Ltd for providing Pyrex and other cookware.
Habasco International Ltd for the loan of basketware.
Stent (Pottery) Ltd for the loan of glazed pottery oven-
to-table ware.

Compiled by Judith Ferguson
Photographed by Peter Barry
Designed by Philip Clucas and Sara Cooper
Recipes Prepared for Photography by
Jacqueline Bellefontaine